The Holy Verses
By
Olusheyi Banjo

The Holy Verses
By Olusheyi Banjo

Foreword

This book has been a major undertaking for me. It has actually take me 1 year and a half to plan the book. Another six months to decided what I wanted to write and interpret about in each book. But it only took me 2 months (stops and starts included) to actually complete the book. These poems are my interpretations of the Holy Bible, book by book. Some poems are very lengthy, most are short and get straight to the point. In this book I write poetic verses on most of the books from Genesis to Revelations. I write about the beginning of the world according to the holy scriptures to every transition in between. I hope that you enjoy reading this book as much as I enjoyed creating it. God Bless you.

Acknowledgements

I want to say thank you to my heavenly father God, Jesus and The holy spirit for giving me the inspiration to write and complete this book. I also want to acknowledge every person that has believed in me and that has rocked with me during my journey of life. I love every single one of you.

Dedication

I dedicate this book to my 3 sunshines, my grandchildren Carla Patricia, Deshawn Jr. and little Issac.Pop loves each and every one of you. Also dedicate this book to my wonderful godson Devonte Duke James. I love you so much and I am so proud of you.

The World Begins (Genesis)
The World began with just words
The most important words
Let there be light
From the light,which God saw was good,
he created the whole world and every living thing in it, including his most important creation
Man and Woman
Mighty Most High God Yahweh created this wonderful world in 6 whole days
No more no less
He saw that everything was blessed
Then that ole beguiling serpent had to ruin God's perfect plan
God's perfect plan for man
Tempted Adam tempted Eve
And they gave on in
And that's how sin was to begin
Then their child Cain did the ugliest thing
Murdered his brother Able because he had the better offering
He was kicked out of the presence of the most high
I know that he wanted to die
The world kept going and going down it's path
They tried to build a heavenly tower
I know that made God laugh
So he went down and confused their language
So that each other they couldn't understand
What was and is wrong with man
Then they became more wicked
Wickedness grew
Until it made God sorry and he grieved too
So sorry was he
that he decided to destroy everyone accept Noah and his family
Noah built that ark despite the haters and the folks
Him and his family were saved from the world's terrible fate
Isn't God great
Then we see Father Abraham and his righteousness
He believed God in everything including the promise of a son
He held on though he did waiver a bit
But he held strong and saw God fulfill his promise through it
Then we see Isaac his son grow strong

With his 2 sons they got along.
Then his son Jacob who was the father of tithe 12 tribes
Because of them we are alive
His son Joseph kept them all alive when famine was in the land
God lifted Joseph above his brothers with his mighty and high hand
He went through so much yet he became a blessing to everyone of his family
That's what we all need to be
So my children that's the story of how the world began

The Exit From Egypt (Exodus)
Moses was a great man,chosen by God
Chosen to lead God's people from Pharaohs land
He was a mighty man
A prince of Egypt,a great and Godly man
The only one since Adam who saw God face to face and lived
There came a day when God saw his chosen people crying
And he said "I wanna deliver them from their oppressors
From their transgressors"
So God used mighty Moses and his brother Aaron to tell Pharaoh the truth
But ole stubborn Pharoah refused to listen
So God had to show him the deal
Show him the almighty God is real
He sent the plagues of locus,blood and frogs
He sent the plagues of live stock that even killed the hogs
But none of that got to mean ole Pharoah
Until the plague where his son died
Then he let the Israelites go
Let them go for sho
But he then changed his mind again and decided to chase
But God again had to show his face
Parted the Red Sea and Pharoah's men stowed
God made them drown
Yes God is mighty,be even gave his people commandments and laws to follow
Those laws were not Hollow
That's the exit of God's people from Egypt

Priestly Rules (Leviticus)
These are the rules the priestly rules
The rules that the priest and people must follow
Every priest must be sanctified before coming into the holy of holies
Every one must offer their best sacrifice
Everyone must give a tenth of their grain and goods as a sin offering
Purify yourself before the day of sacrifice
Uncleanness cannot be found in you
You must live according to God's rules
His way
Do it today
So many more rules
Too many to write
AND
These are the rules the priestly rules
Which are written in this book

Count My People (Numbers)
How many are my people
Too many to count
But we will try
The children of Israel are numerous
The tribe of Dan
The tribe of Issacar
The tribe of Benjamin
The Tribe of Reuben
The tribe of Judah
The tribe of Joseph
The tribe of Gad,
The Tribe of Asher
The tribe of Levi
The tribe of Naphtali
The tribe of Sin son
And the tribe of Ephraim
These are the tribes
The Israelite tribes
Too numerous to count
Teach me lord to count my people

Moses' Farewell (Deuteronomy)
Gather around my children
Oh children of Israel
And I will read you this letter
Moses final letter to you
Be strong oh Israel
Because you have a great battle ahead of you
Remember the Lord your God in all that you do
Take the ark of the covenant and Joseph's bones too
Fight the good fight with courage and conviction
Never forget the God of your fathers
Nor the love of your mothers
My children be strong and spiritual
Oh children of Israel remember what Moses taught you always

Jericho Battle (Joshua)
We're gonna march down the walls of Jericho
Said we're gonna march down the walls of Jericho
We're gonna march around the wall 7 times
Said we're gonna march around the wall 7 times
'Until we conqueror that city
We'll victoriously conqueror that city
That city in the promised land
Led by our great leader Joshua
We're led by the great Joshua
God will give us our home flowing with milk and honey too
It's flowing with milk and honey too
We've made it to our new home through and through
said we've made it to our new home through and through
our new home in Jericho

Judged by The Judges(Judges)
Before there were kings in Israel, there were Judges
Judges to decide what was right and fair between the Israelites
Judges who decided what was wrong and what was right
There was Deborah,Abdon Othniel, Ehud, Gideon, Shamgar too
Tola, Jair, Jephthah, Ibzan,Elon,
And don't forget the mighty warrior Samson
Each one has done great deeds for Israel
Each one used by God
Each one God chose himself
They were the might Judges
The Judges of Israel

Tender Love (Ruth)
I lost a love not knowing God's plan
THat he had someone great
A greater love for ,me
God has a sense of humor sometimes
He sets your disappointments and heartbreaks up so that his greater plan can be revealed for your life
My first husband died in my native land
then my father and brother in law died as well
It was just me, my sister n law and mother in law left all alone
My sister in law left so it was me and my mother
i chose to stay with her because he was like my mother
I had to go to work to make money to feed us both
That's when God's plan was unleashed
he led me to my new love
my new life
The reliever of my strife
now we're in love and married too
i have a new son Obed,God's plan worked through and through
and I am the great-grandmother of a future King
God's ways are so wonderful and so clean

Samuel (I Samuel)
There once was a great prophet
Prophet of Israel named Samuel
He was a hearer of the Lord's voice
A seer of visions
The last of the great judges of Israel
The annointer of 2 great kings
From the time he was born he knew the Lord
He loved the Lord
he first heard the Lord at a very young age
and he kept hearing the Lord until the day he was no more
He was a great man a witness to God's greatness
God's might, when David killed the mighty Goliath
Samuel was God's mediator to his people
Samuel was a mighty mighty man of God

King David (1 & 2 Samuel)
Mighty King David
A man after God's own heart
Started as a shepherd boy tending his father Jesse's flock
Then God chose him above his brothers to become Israel's second king
He killed the giant Goliath with rocks and a sling
He comforted the raging spirit of King Saul
Made friends with Jonathan Saul's main son
He was loved by all the children Israel,even when King Saul tried to hunt him down and attack
Then after Saul died David became Israel's most mighty King
He reigned with fairness and justice
But mighty King David was still just a man
Who had 1 flaw, he loved a wife of another
Took her and made her his
Then killed the man to keep her
But from that sin he did not relish
He rose back up and continued his reign
Even when his own son Absalom tried to attack
God had King David's back
Much to King David's dismay
His son died on the way
But no matter what King David was a mighty mighty man and a Godly man

Wisdom(1 Kings)
Lord I ask that you give me wisdom to lead your people
Please give me wisdom to be wise in all things
That I may judge the children of Israel the way that you want me to
I want to be a great king for you
King Solomon prayed that prayer
Then he became the wisest and richest king
That Israel ever had
So I'm praying the same prayer lord
Make me wise
Not just wise in my own eyes
But wise for you
To do the wise thing always
Lord please give me wisdom
Like you gave King Solomon

Tell Me The History(2 Kings 1&2 Chronicles)
Tell me the history, the history of Israel's kings
The history of Israel from the kings to their exile
From King David to King Nebuchadnezzar
Tell me about the great wars
The great deeds of the good kings
How God overthrew the evil kings
How God divided the kingdom of Israel from Solomon's son
How King Solomon turned away from God,after his concubines
How God gave the children of Israel to their enemies
Tell me the history,the holy history

Rebuild The Temple (Ezra)
Now that we have been delivered from Babylonian exile
Let us rebuild the temple
The temple to honor our God
To worship the God of our fathers
To honor our deliverer
Brothers and sisters let us sanctify and purify ourselves before the Lord
Let us pray together on one accord
God of heaven,let us be not weary
Even though our enemy king Cyrus wants to stop us
Let us build your temple to honor you
And God delivered us from King Cyrus
He raised up King Radius,to allow us to rebuild
Brothers and sisters now that we are free
Let us rebuild the temple to honor our God

Set Things Right (Nehemiah)
I am a cupbearer to the Persian King Artaxerxes
I was brought here to set things right
We are going to rebuild the walls of Jerusalem
We are going to rebuild our native land
I know you all are not happy with our government
But brothers and sisters Lets live in peace
The God of our fathers would not want us to wage war
Let us be on 1 accord
Brothers and sisters let us do this for God
And let us set things right

Queen Esther (Esther)
You are a chosen beauty of your people
You are as lovely as a spring day
You are wise yet lovely
Chosen to bring joy to your people
Chosen to tell the king a harsh truth
Queen Esther Queen Esther
Beautiful and wise
Queen Esther Queen Esther
Chosen by God to bring truth in a world of lies
Queen Esther Queen Esther
No other queen will compare
Queen Esther Queen Esther
God truly had his hand on you

     OLUSHEYI BANJO

This Test (Job)
God told Satan my servant Job you can test
I know that whatever you do he will not go against me at all
So I'm in this test trying to survive
Trying to stay alive
My children are gone,most of my worldly goods too
I don't know what else I can do
My wife and friends tell me just curse God and die
I don't listen to their words or hear their lies
I'm determined to stay true to my God and his plan
I'm determined to stand
Though the movers may mock
The scoffers may scoff
The people may doubt that God has his almighty hand on me
I will win with the master
I didn't give in
And in the end I got everything that was taken from me back
Thank you Lord I survived Satan's attack

I wanna Sing A Song (Psalms)
Lord I wanna sing a song of praise to you
I wanna sing of your mighty works
Also how good you've been to me
You've been my protection
You've been my healer
Been my best friend
When I was uncertain you gave me surety
When I was lost your amazing grace found me
You are my champion
You are my creator
The one who knows me best
It will take me forever to sing my song of praise to you

Wise Words (Proverbs)
Wise words written by King Solomon
Wise words to live by
Honor God and yourself
As well as people around you
My son do what is right 24-7
That's the only way you'll make it to heaven
Honor your body
For God almighty is watching everything that you do
Find a virtuous woman,make her your wife
She will bring you joy through your life
Wisdom is to be treasured above every dollar
Even silver and gold
Wisdom will be with you even when you get too old
These and so much more are the jewels of wisdom that King Solomon wrote
They will forever be
Wise words written by Solomon
Wise words to live by

Preach On Preacha (Ecclesiastes)
Preach on preacha, preach the word of God
Preach on preach,preach it with conviction and fervor
Tell us to love our neighbors
Preach to us about the times and there is a season
Preach to us,give us the reason
Why would should serve God and follow his way
Why we should forsake vanity every day
Preach on, not just you want us to give and shout
Preach it so we know what living right is about
Preach to us about God almighty and his saving grace
And how we must live right to see his face
Preach on preacha,like a true man of God
Preach on Preacha,and we will listen

Love Me (Songs Of Solomon)
I've been wanting you since the first time I saw you
I've been wanting you to love me
Make me scream your name
Give me the treat you know I deserve
I'm excited just thinking about you
I'll make you excited too
Give me your best
I'll give you mine
There is nothing like the passion that we'll elude
Kiss me while you're in me
Talk dirty to me
Yes,i'm your nasty thing
I'm excited thinking about you
Oh please lover
Love me

God Will Redeem Us(Isaiah)
The most high God has a plan
A divine master plan
To save us once and for all from our sins
Oh Israel
Children of Israel
Get ready for the messiah
Immanuel,Prince Of Peace,God with us, Yeshua, Jesus Christ
He will bring us back to our heavenly father God Yahweh
He will be born pure no stain of sin
Born to a holy Virgin
He will be the healer and restored of many
He will be called miracle worker
Hosanna in the highest
He will feed our body and our souls
But then he will make the ultimate sacrifice
He will sacrifice his precious life
Just like an innocent lamb is a blood sacrifice
He will die a physical death for 3 days
But then he will rise again with all power and glory in his hands
Then ascend back to the father in heaven
Oh children of Israel that's God's divine plan to redeem us

Jeremiah (Jeremiah)
Known by God
Prophet since he was a boy
Prophet of Judah's destruction at the hands of Babylon
Was imprisoned then set free
Wanted for execution because he spoke the true word of God
King Jehoiakim tossed his prophecy into the fire
King Zedekiah gives people permission to kill him, then saves him
Was an outcast for being real
Accused God of abandoning him
Cursed the day he was born
But all of his prophecies came true
In the end Jeremiah wins,but the disobedient hard
headed children of Israel loose
But God Still loves them and offers words of love and comfort to
them
Jeremiah a true man of God

Weeping For My People (Lamentations)
Oh my people I weep for you
Your hard heartedness
Your hard headedness
Your refusal to follow God's way
You going against God's rules
How you disobey God so freely
Thinking of no consequences
But there is a day coming
Where you will weep too
Your cries will drown out the laughter
Your tears will fall like the rain on the ground
Oh listen my people
Heed me before too late
Don't ostracize me
Embrace me
Hear God's word
But you know refuse
So I must continue to weep for my people

You Cheated On Me (Ezekiel)
Lady Israel you cheated on me
Said you cheated on me
Now I want my revenge
Yes I want my revenge
You unfaithfully turned away from me to another lover who you thought could treat you better
But instead it left you empty and hollow
Now it's time for me to destroy you
Yes I'm going to destroy you
Make you really sorry
You are so sorry
You will regret all that you've done to me
After you see your evil ways
I'm sure you will come back to me
Yeah you'll come back
But I love you so much that I will take you back
Yes I'll take you back
You cheated on me lady Israel but I still love you

My God Can Do It (Daniel)
My God is able,yes he is Able
Able to deliver me from the lion's den
Able to stand with me in the fire
Able to hold be down when folks lie and hate on me
I pray to him everyday
And he always makes a way
I have the faith of Daniel and the Hebrew boys
He will,like he's done before
Yes he'll open all blocked doors
My God is almighty
All powerful
He can do anything except lie,fail, and change
My God,yes my God can do it for you, just like he does for me.

You Must Go (Jonah)
If God almighty tells you to go to a block or a city
You must go
If he tells you to preach to the awful sinner
You must preach
If he tells you to give to the undesirable
You must give
Don't be like our brother Jonah,go at his first command
Forsake yourself,even forsake the naysaying man
Go go go
Don't get swallowed up by a giant whale
Let God's will prevail
In the end God's will,will be done
So do it the first time
Whatever God tells you to do
You must do
And
You must go

Minor Prophets (Hosea, Joel, Amos, Obadiah, Micah, Nahum, Habakkuk, Zephaniah, Haggai, Zechariah)

Each one spoke of God's love

They spoke of God's anger for the unfaithfulness of the children of Israel

They spoke of the future coming messiah

Jesus Christ

His redeeming power

He will bring us back to our heavenly father God

The lamb of God

Israel will reject him

But he will be the savior of many

Come back to God is what they all will say

Hosea, Joel, Amos, Obadiah, Micah, Nahum, Habakkuk, Zephaniah, Haggai, Zechariah

They were messengers of God,his judgement and his love for his people Israel

You Can't Cheat God (Malachi)

No matter what you do
  You can't cheat God
  Even if you try
  God will get what is due to him
  Your praise,your tithes and even your time
  It's no use trying to cheat God
  It will not work out well for you
  So submit before you get humbled
  God loves you but he also will humble you
  My children you must remember your creator
  And know that
  You can't cheat God no matter what

The Messiah is Here (Matthew)

Hallelujah the promise of God has been fulfilled
Fulfilled in Jesus Christ
The messiah is here
He was born in a humble circumstance
He ministered to hurting,the broken, the unfit
He healed and raised those who were lame,blind,broken and dead
Fed the 5,000 with 2 fish and 5 loaves of bread
He was about his father's business
He walked on water
Was proclaimed as the ultimate teacher
He gave us a beautiful gift
His precious life
To save us all
To reedem us Back to the father
His sacrifice,his life was awesome
We thought it was finished but
3 days later He rose with all power in his hands
He has become the true and living messiah
Conquered the devil and demons in the fire
Jesus is the messiah forevermore
He's got the keys to all doors
Hallelujah the messiah is here and he is here forever and ever

Miracle Worker (Mark)

He's a miracle worker
Yes he works miracles
He's a miracle worker
He worked a miracle in me
He gave the blind sight
Healed the lame and deaf
Turned water into wine

Healed a woman with an issue of blood
Raised the dead on many occasions
He deserves a standing ovation
He's a miracle worker
Yes he is
Fed the 4,000 and the 5,000 too
Jesus Christ can make a miracle for you
He also forgave the sins of many,that's a miracle
Oh yes
They called him master,teacher messiah
He took the keys from the devil in hell's fire
He healed my body like only he could
Jesus Christ to me is so good
He's a miracle worker
Oh yes he is
Jesus Christ is an awesome miracle worker

Yes Lord (Luke)
Yes Lord

I believe everything that you say
    Yes Lord
    Have your own way
    Yes Lord
    Only you were born of a virgin Mary in Bethlehem
    At 12 was teaching and speaking with the elders in the synagogue
    Told the 12 that you would make them fishers of men
    Gave us heavenly rules,while we are hear on earth
    Spoke words of such beauty
    Even though some hated
    That was just apart of your plan
    Your plan to redeem the summer man
    Yes Lord
    Yes to your way
    Yes Lord
    I'll do everything that you say

Jesus Christ Is The Word (John)
He was there in the beginning when God said let there be light
He helped create man in God's image
He saw that man needed redemption,so he became flesh
He spoke the word and it was so
His words had power
His words were wonderful
He spoke to Lazarus and he got up
He healed the adulterous woman from her sin just by his words
His words are heavenly teachings the parables
He spoke the beattitudes that we all must follow
His love was in his actions and his words too
With his words his life was sacrificed for me and you
Now he's on the right hand of the father
He conquered all
With his words and actions
That"s why Jesus Christ is the true and living word

Holy Spirit Come On In (Acts)
Holy Spirit Come on in
Make yourself at home
Holy Spirit come on in
With you our souls won't roam
Holy Spirit come on in
Saturrate our our souls
Holy Spirit come on in
With you we are whole
Holy Spirit come on in
Fill our souls with peace
Holy Spirit come on it
In your presence evilness will cease
Holy Spirit come on in
Touch our hearts and minds today
Holy Spirit come on it
Make it all okay

We Are All Sinners (Romans)

We are all sinners every single one of us
    We are all unrighteous not one is better than the other
    You might sin differently than me but You're still a sinner too
    We are saved by the grace and mercy Of God almighty
    We sin daily in our thoughts,our deeds and even in our words
    So brothers and sisters don't look down on someone who does things
that you don't do
    Love them anyway
    Treat them well
    Like you wanna be treated
    And remember
    We all sinners
    Some saved by grace

Love Is Liberating(1 Corinthians)

Love is liberating
  Sets your mind and soul free
  Puts your heart at ease
  Doesn't chain you down with demands
  Love understands
  Love doesn't just want for itself
  It gives
  Love lives
  Love is caring
  Love is more than sweet kisses
  Sweet misses
  Love is the strongest power in the universe
  Love makes you strong when life makes you weak
  Love is unconditional
  More than just sexual
  Love real genuine agape love liberates everyone

Love and Unity(2 Corithians)

We need love and Unity
    Gotta bring back the family
    We need love and Unity today
    We need love and Unity
    need to be one for all of us to live in peace
    Put down your guns
    put down your sticks
    Put down the knives
    let go of the bricks
    Give each other love
    stop all the hating
    Stop all this crazy debating
    teach the children that unity is key
    for the survival of the human family
    My brother my sister
    heed the call
    before it's too late and we all fall
    We gotta lift each other up instead of put down
    Or the human race will cease to be around
    Stop before we're all extinct
    Come on y'all just Live in pink
    Time to take to the streets
    And form a love chain that greets
    Don't matter about the president
    what matters the unity of residents
    Black White brown pink and gray
    Time to live in unity today
    Time to say no to crookedness
    Time to live in bliss
    We can make it happen

Yes we sure can
Woman child and man
Get up before it's too late only you can stop this hate
Check your self
Check it right
Get up today
tonight

Stay Close to God (Galatians)

Stay close to God,never turn away
    Never let anybody make you give up on him no way
    Stay close to God,hold to his unchanging hand
    Remember to put him above every man
    Stay close to God,like a friend or a brother
    Treat him sacred like a lover
    Stay close to God and never ever let go
    Stay close and love him so
    Stay close to God in these crazy changing times
    Stay close to God hold on to him like the rich hold on to their dimes
    You'll never regret it
    You'll never feel bad
    You'll never ever be sad
    If you
    Stay close to God with your mind body soul and strength

Obey (Ephesians)

It says obedience is better than sacrifice

That is so true

You've got to obey somebody in your life

You've got to obey your parents or those who guard and protect you when you're young

You've got to obey the law of the the land so that you won't get into costly trouble

You've got to obey your boss or wherever you work,so that you will be paid for it

You've got to obey the rules of wherever you live so that you can continue to live in peace

You've also got to obey God,so that you will gain your eternal reward

In life no matter what

You've got to obey somebody some time

Rejoice Always (Philippians)

Rejoice always because your victory is near
    Let your victory shout ring loud and clear
    Dance and rejoice with all your might
    Get your praise on tonight
    Sing a song of rejoicing and joyfulness
    Be thankful to the most high God because you are blessed
    You are victorious in everything you do
    Don't let the enemy fool you
    More than conquerors more than blessed
    You are the victorious winner in all tests
    Rejoice always even when it doesn't look good
    Cause that's what every believer should
    Let praise continuously be in your mouth
    Never ever entertain doubt
    I'll say it one more time
    We must
    Rejoice always no matter what

Spiritual (Colossians)

Going higher in life
    Going on a spiritual plane
    no longer bound by man
    Living the way the Lord wants me to
    Doin' what he says do
    Denying the flesh and doing what he wants me to
    Living spiritual
    living in the word
    Hallelujah I'm living spiritual
    I'm/living spiritual
    no longer in the natural
    I'm living spiritual
    going higher
    higher in the spiritual
    Fasting and praying
    doing what the Lord say
    Treating my neighbor right
    Doing what the Lord tells me to do
    Instead of doing what I really want to
    No longer listening to my flesh
    For the spiritual/I press
    Daily going higher In God
    That's all I want To do
    I walk by faith not by sight
    I do what the Lord tells me to do everyday
    Instead of doing what my flesh says to do
    For the flesh is contrary to the spirit
    And I wanna build my spirits up
    because I wanna be closer to my God
    I'm living spiritual

Growing In Faith (1 Thessalonians)

When test and trials come you build me up
    You give me awesome strength Lord
    As I read and I learn of your precious word, my faith builds up and
up Lord
    I'm growing stronger in faith and the knowledge of Jesus Christ
    Day by Day I trust in your light
    When my bills were pilling,I couldn't see my way
    Darkness was all around me
    I held to your word and my faith
    You showed what you could do yes
    Brothers and sisters,no matter what we go through
    We gotta grow stronger and stronger in faith
    Day by Day
    If we have no trials
    We have no testimony
    That's why we gotta keep on going
    Keep on growing
    stronger and stronger in faith
    And everything will work out y'all
    God bless you

Be Prepared For The End Times (2 Thessalonians)

The end is near
Probably nearer than you think
Don't you see the signs
Folks claiming to be God.
Crooked preachers
Crooked members
Crooked government
Killing is at an all time high
Love is fleeting
Lust rules
Folks aren't loyal anymore
Say they love you
But they will betray you in a second
That's why we gotta stand firm
Just like the apostle Paul said
Hold on to God's pure word
Only his word won't pass away
Be steadfast
Don't move
Fast and Pray
Don't give up on faith or on God
And
Be prepared for these end times

Pastoral Advice (1 Timothy)

Young man please listen to me
    Heed my words
    Don't let anyone tell you that you're not strong because you are young
    Don't let them hate on you young brotha
    Stand strong in your faith
    Stand strong in your convictions
    You are God's soldier,never forget that
    You must be a light for this dark generation
    There will be times when you question your faith
    There will be times when you are falsely accused
    When you are misused
    And even feel like you are being abused
    That's the time that you've gotta hold on
    That's the time you gotta tell the enemy "Get on
    Outta here"
    You've got to be clear
    You must be consise
    You must be sure of your calling
    You must be unshakeable
    Unbreakable
    You must pray and fast
    Do what the Lord asks
    Stand up my young brother
    And need
    This pastoral advice

Run The Race (2 Timothy)

Run the race with courage and faith
Run the race to see his face
Run the race with integrity and honesty
Run the race with humility
Run the race with pride and conviction
Run the race with diction
Don't try to run the race too fast
For only what you do for Christ will last
Don't try to be better than folks or try to make others feel low
Because I guarantee that is where you will go
Run the race and you will win
If God is running with you until the end

Never Turn Away (Titus)

This world may be going crazy
    This world may be turning away from you Lord
    This world may be saying there's no God
    But i'm gonna tell you that I will never give up on you
    I'll never turn away
    Lord i'll never turn away from you
    I appreciate everything that you are
    Everything that you do
    Who you are
    That's why i'm never turning away

May God Bless You(Philemon)

As you go on your journey in this life
　　May he guide your every step
　　May you not cry in vain
　　May his loving arms surround
　　May Your heart never be down
　　May he bless you with success
　　May you excel in everything that you do
　　May many lives be touched by you
　　May you go far and your future be bright
　　Walk in the light
　　May God bless you with a long and beautiful life

Faithful Assurance (Hebrews)

We have an assurance. a faithful assurance
    That things always work out if Jesus is our guide
    A faithful assurance that God is on our side
    We can face the storms and trials that life will bring
    That God will give a faithful song to sing
    God will supply and provide
    He will never hide
    With works and faith we can conquer it all
    The great and the small
    We have a wonderful faithful assurance
    That God is with us

Live Bold Christian Life (James)

Be bold
Live right
Do what God says do
Walk steadfast
Be the light in the dark and twisted generation
Stand up for God
Let your faith be made know
Don't hide it
Don't be ashamed of it
Proudly proclaim it
Let the world know who's your are
A child of the most high King
The owner of all things
Victory is always assured when you're walking with Jesus Christ
The one who gives and sustains life
Be proud to be a believer
Walk with your head held high
Don't be shy
Live a bold Christian life

Overcomer(1 Peter)

Overcoming
> I'm an overcomer
> Through the struggles and the strife
> The trials and tribulations of life
> I keep overcoming
> Overcomer
> Keep on goin'
> because of Christ
> Thank you lord
> for my life
> The life of a an overcomer

False Prophet (2 Peter)

Should've known you were a wolf in sheep's clothing
    All you care about is the dollar
    You don't love God's people , you try to pimp then
    Hell is reserved for you
    You're an undercover too, that's the worst kind
    Should've laid you out when you threatened to beat me up
    You're a punk and not of God at all
    You're lucky I Haven't called the feds on you, for trying to get me to
pay for something not right
    You wouldn't even sign my pastoral recommendation letter
    Feel sorry for you church members and everyone who is associated
with you
    Because you're a false prophet

Let's Love One Another (1 John)

There's too much hatin on each other these days
Too much jealousy
Too much competition
Too much backbiting
Let's take a break from the hate
Lets love one another
Really love one another
Brotherly and sisterly love
The way God wants us to
Stop trying to vilianize your people
Let the spirit of God's love rule
Embrace instead of chase
them away
Why can't we do it today
Everyone is important in God's eyes
Everyone needs to be loved and cherished
Taken the time to lift up
Instead of tear down
Be an lover instead of a fighter
Brothers and sisters we need to love one another

Abide In Truth (2 John)

Live in it
Cherish it
Walk in it
Let yourself be immersed in it
Keep your mind and heart stayed on it
Never let lies or the father of lies be your friend
Love it like you love a lover
Stay close to it
Let it be in your tunnel vision
Don't let it cause division
Always let it be your lamp
Don't let it cramp
It will fight your battle and win
Keep it along with integrity
Everybody just abide in truth

Do Good (3 John)

Life is full of crazy evil things
    Crazy evil people
    That's why you're got to do good
    Do the right thing always
    Be the general of the good army
    Treat your neighbor with kindness and love
    Go out of your way to be good
    Go above and beyond the call of duty
    Be the difference that people see
    When folks try to do evil turn it around
    and do good
    You just might change an evil heart
    You just might fix someone who's falling apart
    Go head and do good

Be Real (Jude)

In a world full of fakes
 In a world full of shakes
 In a world full of snakes
 Just quake
 The crazy system
 The weird times
 No carbon copy
 No being sloppy
 No hypocrisy
 No heresy
 just be real

Jesus Christ Is Coming Soon (Revelations)

Don't you see the signs
    Can't you tell
    Nation against nation
    Brother against sister
    Mothers throwing away and murdering their own children
    Father's raping their seed
    Church against church
    Preacher against preacher
    So called men of God acting like the devil himself
    Government officials are 100% crooked
    The prophecies are being fulfilled daily
    Oh I can't wait for Jesus Christ to come back
    Come back in all of his glory
    All of his splendor
    Riding high on the clouds to take us home
    Home with him in glorious heaven
    After he defeats the great beast
    The beast that will rise up and terrorize the saints
    After the great battle, he and the angels will fight and win
    Satan and his demons will cast down to their eternal punishment in
the everlasting lake of fire
    The anti-Christ will be thrown down with Satan
    Their will be a glorious shout from the present saints and the ones
that have gone before
    The 24 elders of the church will cry
    Holy Holy Holy to the lamb of God
    Who defeated the evil one once and for all
    We will sing a victory song
    New heaven new earth
    We will finally see our heavenly father God face to face

We will live with him and the angels
Paradise with no ending
Only beautiful beginnings
I will be reunited with my father,great-grandmother and every loved one who has gone before
Love and peace will surround us like never before
On that wonderful resurrection day
When Jesus Christ comes back
One More For Reader 11 (poem)
We went on a spiritual biblical journey
From Genesis to Revelations
And every book in between.
I gave my interpretation of the holy scriptures
I hope that you loved them
I hope you gained something spiritual from them
I hope that you enjoyed reading them as much as I enjoyed creating them
Stay rooted and grounded until we meet again
Let love peace and God be your guide
Until we meet again stay shining